MW01329656

This Journal Belongs To:

Made in the USA
Middletown, DE
06 April 2024

52545553R00076